A Cat Called
Scratcher

Linda West

First published in 2023 by Paragon Publishing, Rothersthorpe

Illustrations: © Dan Dumbarton

ISBN 978-1-78792-007-1

Book design, layout and production management by Into Print
www.intoprint.net
+44 (0)1604 832149

For

Chris, Joshua, Dan, Tracy, my Children, Grandchildren, Great Grandchildren, not forgetting the kindness of Spartan-Warrior.

CONTENTS

Scratcher Learns A Lesson

The whiskers of naughty Scratcher are as bushy as his tail
He's the colour of chalky charcoal, and a very bossy male.
He prowls around the house; he thinks he owns the place
Please stay out of his way, or he'll hiss straight in your face!

He's known for scaring rabbits; he thinks it's so much fun
To chase them round the garden, run rabbits run.
And when he sees Puss next door, Puss will hide himself away
Naughty Scratcher steals his food, he does this every day.

And now Puss is so skinny, he can barely leave the house
Scratcher doesn't care; he's off to chase a mouse!
But this is not all he does; he's far naughtier than that
When Grandma comes for tea, he wees right in her hat!

Scratcher thinks it's really funny, to make Grandma cry
The naughty cat doesn't care, he just spits in her eye.
OH! NO! thinks angry Grandma, it's time to get real tough
I've warned him about his naughtiness; I've really had enough!

She's going to give Scratcher away, would anyone like a cat?
Grandma loved him really, she was far too kind to do that
So she went to find some help, to change Scratcher's naughty way
They all listened very quietly to what Grandma had to say.

The only way to teach Scratcher is for him to learn to be good,
A taste of his own medicine, of course we can – we could!
They knew it wouldn't be easy, for Scratcher is no fool
He enjoys being naughty, not sticking to the rule!

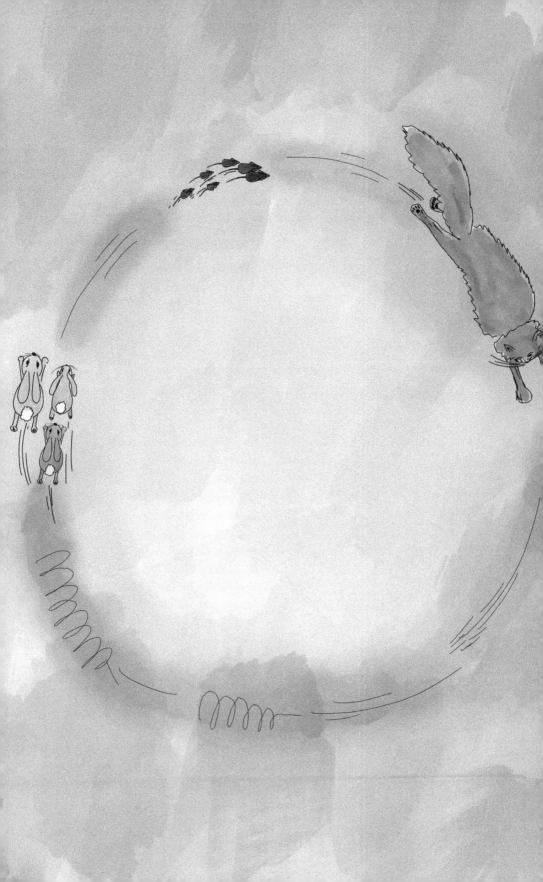

So between them all they made a plan, the rabbits and all alike
The next time Scratcher was naughty,
everyone would need to fight…
At first Scratcher was angry when the rabbits stood their ground
They no longer ran away, they chased him, round and round.

Scratcher made a quick escape; his game no longer fun
Teasing the fluffy rabbits, he knew what he'd become.
Oh my, I've been a bully, a thief and a spiteful cat
Almost starving Puss to death, there was no need for that!

So Scratcher is now listening, he's learnt to purr instead of spit
His tail is still as bushy, and his whiskers are still as thick
He's been kinder to the rabbits, kept away from the mouse's hole
Stopped stealing Puss's food, to be good is his winning goal!

He's learning to change his behaviour; it will take him a little while
He's trying hard to be a good cat and really change his style
He's stopped making Grandma cry, and he's done all she said
And no longer wees in her hat; he now wees in Grandpa's instead!

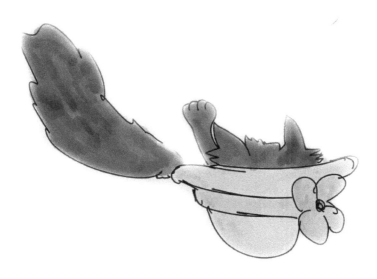

Scratcher's Reward

Scratcher's been trying very, very hard to be a really good cat
He's stopped stealing Puss' food and weeing in Grandpa's hat!
He's not chasing the rabbits; he's almost become their friend
And Grandma is pleased with him, but wait the story doesn't end

Life has become boring; yawn, Scratcher's so tired of being good
He thinks he might go out tonight; to find the "Cat in the Hood"
Now the "Cat in the Hood" is very naughty,
and is known to steal meat
She has a big reward on her head:

cooked chicken, all you can eat!

Now this impressed Scratcher, his tummy rumbled at the thought
What if he could win the reward without getting himself caught?
Chicken was his favourite meat; it would be a great surprise
He would share the chicken with Grandma, and not spit in her eye!

So off he went late one night and found the "Cat in the Hood"
What are you doing here Scratcher; I heard you were being good?
Scratcher lifted his tail high and fiddled with his bushy whiskers
"Cat in the Hood" meowed loudly; he was circled by her sisters!

I want to be in on your robbery, "Cat in the Hood" let him stay
"There's some chicken up for grabs, ok you're in,
and it's your lucky day."
Wow! thought Scratcher that was far easier than I thought
I will give the police the address; *Hee Hee* the gang will get caught!

I will claim the chicken reward and take it home for tea
But the "Cat in the Hood" kept it quiet, smirked. "Come with me"
Scratcher joined the gang of cats – *OH NO*, it's Grandma's Street!
The "Cat in the Hood" pushed Scratcher,
GO ON, STEAL THE MEAT!

Scratcher's bushy whiskers twitched, this wasn't to be the plan
A loud **BANG** made them jump; Scratcher looked for the gang
He had hold of the chicken, *OH NO!* What will Grandma say?
She'll send him to the police station; it was not his lucky day!

And then like magic, Grandma arrived,
rescued him from the ground
The "Hood and The Gang" ran away, Scratcher froze,
made no sound
What are you doing Scratcher, mixing with those naughty alley cats?
Grandma snatched the chicken; he wanted to wee in her hat!

I thought you were becoming a good boy; *I am*, Scratcher said
Grandma believed him and cooked them chicken before bed.
And now no longer hungry, Scratcher meowed this is not good
Grandma said not to steal; she's as naughty as the "Cat in the Hood"

"Tell me Grandma," asked Scratcher
"why did we eat stolen meat for tea?"
"The chicken wasn't stolen Scratcher,
it was mine, you almost burgled *ME*!"
So Scratcher said "I'm very sorry,
and I know it's naughty to steal meat
I didn't intend to do the robbery;
I just wanted the reward to eat!"

So Grandma gave Scratcher a cuddle and let him sleep inside her hat
He promised he wouldn't wee in it, but no, he did exactly that...

naughty Scratcher!

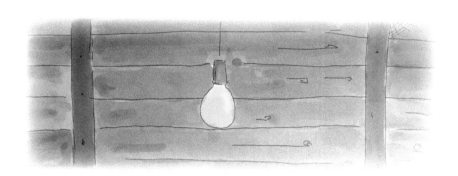

Scratcher's Surprise

Scratcher was sitting on Grandma's lap; her hand stroking his fur
Scratcher loved the attention; he went Purr…Purr…Purr…
But lately he'd noticed Grandma was becoming short of breath
He wanted to surprise her; he very nearly caused her death!

He'd seen some wheels somewhere, yes, he remembered,
in the shed.
He went to find Grandpa's tools, an idea formed in his head
He hoped Grandma would like it; it would be a great surprise
Scratcher found what he needed; he would build it right to size!

Building was a two cat job so he called the cat next door,
Puss was now Scratcher's friend; he starved skinny Puss no more!
"How can I help?" purred Puss, his fluffy ears listened to the plan
The two cats preened their whiskers, and then they soon began…

They worked till they had blisters; their paws were red and sore
But Scratcher knew it would be worth it,
Grandma would love it, for sure!
So when the work was finished, the two cats stood proud and tall
The only thing left to do was give Grandma and Grandpa a call.

Oh No! silently thought Grandpa, when he saw the scary surprise
What was Scratcher thinking of, he had to cover up his eyes!
Grandma absolutely loved it, she jumped on extra quick!
She had her own skateboard; Grandpa thought he might be sick!

Scratcher then joined Grandma, they went whizzing down the street
Grandma's hat went flying, and she almost lost her teeth!
"STOP!" called anxious Grandpa;
"YOU ARE HEADING FOR THE RIVER!"
Both him and Puss went white;
Scratcher and Grandma, all of a quiver!

Down into the murky water, both of them soaking wet
"OH NO!" shouted Puss and Grandpa, "no ambulance here yet!!"
But luckily for Scratcher, Grandma had learnt to swim
And instead of saving Grandma, she surprised and saved him!

They didn't need an ambulance, just a good old drying out
Scratcher preened his bushy whiskers and shook his tail about
Grandma turned out her pockets and looked thoroughly surprised
To see a big colourful rainbow fish
with an *ENORMOUS* pair of eyes

...but that's another story!

Scratcher At The Coronation

"Get out of there" called Grandma, as she shooed Scratcher away
He was pawing the important invite that had arrived for her today
She was going to the King's Coronation, he was new to the thrown
Scratcher's eye's popped out, he didn't want to be home alone!

He fiddled with his bushy whiskers; he would need to make a plan
He wanted to go to the Palace, meet the King and the royal clan!
Scratcher's heart was pounding, and his tail swung high in the air
He would climb inside Grandma's hat, she wouldn't notice him there.

The train to London was busy; Grandma's hat was hot and dry
What if Grandma noticed him, he was slipping over her good eye
Then bish bash, he hit the floor and with fright he weed on a lady
It was Scratcher's lucky day; he could blame it on her baby!

"*AHH!* What are you doing here Scratcher?" cried Grandma,
angry with the cat
Scratcher grinned through his sharp white teeth
"*Oh!* So sorry about that!
But I want to see the King and the famous glittering crown jewels"
"You can't do that Scratcher, that's against the Palace rules!"

We'll see about that thought Scratcher,
as he ran and left Grandma alone
It won't take me long to get there
and take a look at the King's throne.

So sure enough he got there and climbed the high Palace wall
Then he realised he was shaking – what if he would suddenly fall…?
He tried so hard to steady himself; he really needed to be brave
The King wouldn't like a whining cat, but he felt quite afraid
He stuck his claws in tightly but it just wasn't enough

Down …
      down …
           tumbling down …

                  he landed on something rough!

A bag of jewels no less, Scratcher couldn't believe his eyes
"STOP THAT MAN!" shouted someone; "he's told the King lies
He said he'd come to enlarge the crown but he's stolen it instead!"
Scratcher jumped on the burglar's back, and stopped him dead!

Everyone cheered Scratcher, and held him high in the air
Grandma came running over, what a clever, clever pair
For Grandma had spotted the thief and had raised the alarm
Scratcher purred, his tail held high, with such delightful charm!

Then something special happened, the King called out loud
"Who saved my crown jewels?"; he mingled with the crowd
It was us, waved Grandma and Scratcher,
"Then please come with me, try on the glittering crown jewels,
Come and eat some tea."

Scratcher and Grandma were so delighted, tea with the King!
Scratcher couldn't believe his eyes, he even began to sing
Then later on he got to sit on the throne, how excited was he
Oh no! Grandma was right; he wished he'd gone and had a wee!

The End ... for now

Ingram Content Group UK Ltd.
Milton Keynes UK
UKHW052145030423
419585UK00002B/2

A road to recovery from porn and sex addiction – a Christian answer.

ISBN-10: 1092606157

ISBN-13: 978-1092606158

Scripture references are from the following sources:

The Holy Bible: New King James Version © 1982 by Thomas Nelson, Inc. English Standard Version © 2010 by Crossway. New American Standard Bible © 1960, 1962, 1963, 1968, 1971, 1972, 1973, 1975, 1977, 1995 by The Lockman Foundation. New International Version © 1973, 1978, 1984 by Biblica, Inc. The Amplified Bible, Expanded Edition © 1987 by Zondervan and The Lockman Foundation. The Complete Jewish Bible © 1998 by Jewish New Testament Publications, Inc. The Living Bible © 2005 by Tyndale House Publishers, Inc. Good News Bible © 1976 by American Bible Society. The Message © 1993, 1994, 1995 by NavPress.

Contents.

Introduction

From a Christian perspective, we presently live in a very promiscuous society. Biblical values and Christian morals are rapidly undermined in a post-modern world view of secularism. There has emerged a mainstream moral relativism, a philosophy of "anything goes" as long as the mainstream remain unaffected. Such morality has no faith base apart from humanism and a liberal one at that; it sorely lacks a fundamental basis for ethics or morality. This leaves the state, media and mainstream thoughts empowered to determine and even dictate the way society moves forward. Opportunities for inappropriate sexual thoughts and behaviour is freely available, particularly so on the internet and social media. At the time of this writing, statistics showed that sexual crimes were still on the increase.

This road to recovery is open to all Christian's; and, perhaps, it might even help the non-believer. It can also provide some valuable insights to the partner of an addict. If you're not a Christian, then simply ask Jesus to reveal Himself to you and hopefully along this path you will experience that abundant life He has promised all who will trust in Him.

If you have become entangled in the hedge of addiction, then I can assure you there is **hope**. If it is a spouse or good friend to someone who has been caught up in this, then there is **hope**. Freedom lies in knowing Christ. Jesus came and promised, "If the Son sets you free you are free indeed", and, "I have come that you may have life and life abundantly." I wrote this book because I had to find and walk this path, that is why it is *a* path not *the only* path. If it can help you in any way, that would be such a blessing. There are good practical guidelines contained in it, which will help you if you are willing to take them on board.

The first step to recovery is the same as with all other addictions, you have to *understand and accept that your life has become unmanageable* on your own and that you are willing to enlist the help of others to be set free. The **second step** is to *acknowledge that you actually like what you do*, that is the addictive pattern, whatever addiction that might entail. It is **also crucial** to understand that *the power of any addiction lies in its secrecy*, secrecy driven by shame. Shame is different from guilt. Shame entails rejection, and in Scriptural terms, the picture is that of being found naked or dishonoured, whereas guilt has to do with being liable to a charge or action, being indebted. Shame, therefore, makes us fear exposure and rejection, leaving us abandoned and marginalised by other people or society as a whole. Thus, we create "masks" to "cover-up" our weaknesses and failures. By wearing a mask, we believe that in doing so, we regain control over the problem, which of course is a lie. This is widely known as the shame-fear-control cycle and it is fuelled by the secrecy of the addiction(s).

If you are a Christian, the feelings of shame, guilt and despondency will be accompanied with a diminished sense of Holy Spirit's anointing in your life. But you have to understand and know for sure that He will *never* leave you. His power and/or giftings might seem to wane, and experiencing His intimate Presence will be lessened by the addiction in the long run.

The **third step** is that you must acknowledge that *you cannot walk this path on your own*. Independence, trying to cope on your own, from the Christian perspective, is rooted pride and eventually leads into a vicious cycle, because it is maintaining a bad coping strategy to try and prevent the shame of the addiction. The moment you allow others into that area of your life, to co-labour with you on this road to recovery, you will feel as if a great weight has been lifted off your shoulders. A major hindrance or obstacle will have been removed. Remember, even God is in fellowship as the Trinity. As the Body of Christ and as fellow believers we need each other to grow and mature, but also to support one another and help each other to be set free; "Therefore, confess your sins to one another, and pray for one another so that you may be healed." Independence, thinking you can manage this by yourself, will leave you vulnerable and it will make your path more difficult if not impossible. Possible causes, implications and more importantly, the way out, will be made plain in this book.

Some of the causes of addiction:

The causes of a detrimental addiction are most often multifactorial. There are many theories about, but for us, as Christians we know that we take a three-dimensional approach: spirit, soul and body. The approach is holistic and should include all three aspects.

Wikipedia reports that "the two properties that characterize all addictive stimuli are that they are ***reinforcing*** (i.e., they increase the likelihood that a person will seek repeated exposure to them) and ***intrinsically rewarding*** (i.e., they are perceived as being inherently positive, desirable, and pleasurable)." This means that addiction is *not just a psychological*, but it also has a physiological effect on our bodies. The reward cross-sensitization between amphetamine and sexual activity means that ***exposure to one increases the desire for both***, and its process is probably part of the *dopamine dysregulation syndrome*.

Change of mind, right versus wrong thinking:

If you really want something, you will find a way to justify it. They're called "***permission-givers***". In Scripture, the basis and source of all thinking are localised in your heart. Thus, wrong thinking, driven by urges and feelings will lead to wrong premises and actions. *Wrong thinking*, a ***craving for fulfilment*** and in particular the idea that you can fill the gap in your life with immediate, temporary gratification can set one up.

This forms the basis of developing a coping strategy – a good one or a bad one. Addicts invariable develop bad ones that really make them feel better in the short term. Looking for that instant gratification. Yielding to your feelings without thinking things through – not employing consequential thinking – can lead you astray. That is why some Christian psychologists feel that a lack of good parenting can be a very important cause in setting one up for sexual sin; as comfort *and* security are sought in an "alternative" intimacy level, especially true of a father-figure because one lacks the ability to fully connect intimately with Father-God.

It is therefore extremely important to realise that for most addicts; their addiction is the result of a bad "coping strategy" or "coping mechanism". How do you cope?

1. <u>"Sins of the fathers" – your past and your present</u>:

It might be helpful to understand that some factors in your past can set you up (predispose you) and strengthen the root of your addiction. For instance, your society's moral values, your country of upbringing; what were your parents' attitudes towards sex and sexuality? Who were the main mentors in your youth? How did they instil an understanding of love, affection and intimacy? Did any of your parents or grandparents suffer from addictions? Were there any mental health issues in your home? How were you brought up? Have you suffered abuse yourself? In what environment did you grow up? What kind of pressures and peer pressures did you have to face as a child? How did you cope with that? What did your initial sexual imprinting entail (your first sexual exposure and/or experience)? These can go very deep and leave vulnerable areas in your life making it easier to lean towards developing bad coping strategies as well as unhealthy thought patterns, labile feelings and ungodly beliefs. Ungodly beliefs are those things we believe inherently about God, self and others which are wrong (unbiblical) and which can leave a detrimental mark on our lives.

2. Sexual Imprinting:

Another important aspect to consider is your sexual imprinting. This term is used to describe your very first sexual encounter and the lead up to it. The way you experience your first exposure to sex and intimacy generally sets you up for the rest of your life, it will influence all future sexual behaviour. How did you first become sexually aware? For instance, was it a voyeuristic experience, reading pornographic magazines or books, watching pornographic movies, going online and watching pornography, or even novels or newspapers with some sordid encounters? They prime your expectations and create desires for later life. When they are unmet in a later, real relationship, it will fuel the entitlement to your expectations. The lust or desires cultivated previously will be perceived as "lacking", and if the boundaries are not strong, then sexual addiction may ensue. If the first experience was particularly bad, then specific ministering or even therapy might be needed. Consider recognised ministries that can help you like Sozo or Restoring the Foundations or read the book, "An integrated approach to healing" by Chester and Betsy Kylstra.

3. Entitlement:

At the root of the addiction lies instant gratification, selfishness and selfish ambition. It is all about what "I want what I want" and that then translates into "I will". It is very rare to find someone addicted to Broccoli or Brussel sprouts (unless you're pregnant!). **We want what we like and we like what we want**. The urge or desire must underlie the want. This is then driven by entitlement, which means "I deserve a bit of pleasure", "I'm not getting what I'm due, so I'll gratify myself", "I work hard and the pressures are so many", "I deserve an escape" or even "everybody else is getting it, surely I have a right to get it too." These permission-givers will work in close liaison with your strongest coping mechanism.

From God's perspective, our rights should be encapsulated within His plans and will for our life. We are not our own. Christ redeemed us, which means He paid for us with His life, to be reconciled to God. Therefore, our rights and deep desires must be subject to loving and honouring Him. The calling in Christ is simple, but hard to process for an addict. The apostle Paul wrote "Even so consider yourselves to be dead to sin, but alive to God in Christ Jesus. Therefore, do not let sin reign in your mortal body so that you obey its lusts" (NASB). We will all appear before the judgment seat of Christ and we will have to give an account of everything we have said and done here on earth. Paul wrote, "but I discipline my body and make it my slave, so that, after I have preached to others, I myself will not be disqualified" (ESV). The word disqualified, *adikomos*, can also mean "tested but not approved". The only "rights" we have as Christians is to the Tree of Life and to become the children of God. When you realise that you are a child of God, you will understand that your life is subject to the loving rule of Father-God and that humility rather than entitlements are the way to a happy and fulfilling life here and now, as well as forever.

4. Some people and professions are at greater risk:

It is a known fact that people in the caring professions are at greater risk of such addiction. *Doctors, nurses and those in social care or pastoral care.* A reason could be the level of intimacy they're afforded within their profession. This vulnerability is particularly true of their use of the internet and social media, for it affords an opportunity to exercise that entitlement without the setting of the normal boundaries; and, the false sense of doing it alone and in private is a strong factor – "I'm not hurting anyone". In church, the *prophets* are at greater risk too, Pastor Rick Joyner in his book "A Vision for the 20th Century" emphasised that people with a prophetic (seer) calling will be at greater risk, as they have much more "active imaginations" and they have an ability to "see" abstractly more easily; "seeing" in the spirit plays such a vital role in their spiritual and natural life. Anecdotally people on the spectrum with Asperger's Syndrome or high functioning autism will also be predisposed to this kind of addiction. As they find a change of mind very difficult once they are trapped in a destructive pattern of thinking; not unlike like an LP vinyl record that's stuck in a groove going round and round.

What keeps you trapped?

The first and foremost reason is the immediate gratification of going online or looking at pornography. You like it and for a moment, it satisfies, gratifies and fills a hole. Until you identify what else can fill it better, you'll always want to go back to it.

1. *Strong feelings, inappropriate thoughts and bad coping strategies.*

As a coping strategy, watching pornography is a bad one, but it is one nonetheless. If it distracts you and/or fills the need for entitlement, then you'll continue to do it. Until that search for a secure release from stress is met in God, through an authentic encounter with Him as a Person; or, at least find a healthier outlet, you'll desire to go back to what works well, even if it is just for the moment.

Once it becomes a regular thing, you will have developed a preamble or ritual leading into addictive behaviour. This differs from person to person, but you might get an alcoholic drink, go around the house to ensure you're out of sight, or go to a particular place or den, or watch late-night television, or look at magazines. It is important, crucial for the addict to understand: *the ritual(s) and the addiction(s) are closely and inextricably associated with each other, both on an emotional, but also on a physical level.* The "pleasure area" in the brain gets sensitised by the addiction, and "happy" or "excitatory" substances (neurotransmitters) are secreted to stimulate the brain in those areas. *Over a period of time the brain undergoes an important change physically.* It upregulates the receptors, they become more sensitive in those specific areas, you start stimulating the pleasure areas before you even engage in pornography, *the ritual sets you up even before you start to look at pornography.*

It is therefore very important to get effective relapse prevention strategies into place as you emerge from the addiction.

This has two important aspects you need to understand. Once you have identified *the specific triggers that make you vulnerable* to act inappropriately by looking at porn, you must start to avoid or dismantle them. The second thing to realise is that over a period of time *when you choose to avoid the triggers* that lead on to commit the act of looking at porn, *it will become easier to say no over a period of time.* Things will progressively get better and easier. It will take time to down-regulate the receptors and the release of neurotransmitters, but things can and will return to "normal" *in time.* The important lesson to take home is that *the ritual and its associated triggers are just as dangerous as the addiction itself!*

Feelings and **inappropriate thoughts** will lead up to the ritual. Once the urge is there, what are thinking about? Try to identify step one, the feeling and/or thought(s) that sets the ritual and then the addiction into action.

Unfortunately, once we entertain inappropriate thoughts, it becomes easier to objectify. **"The power of internet sex is that it is one step away from reality."**

2. Curiosity!

As creative beings we're naturally curious. There is a healthy curiosity, but if channelled into exploring the internet, it can very easily end up looking at the wrong things. The excitement of discovering *new* porn is a very strong stimulus and keeps the addict's ability to feel aroused alive. This is a strong incentive in keeping the addiction going, despite common sense, for the excitement of something new as part of that ritual is a very, very strong catalyst. Once you realise the strength of such curiosity in your life and while you are web surfing, you can purposefully seek to suppress the urge to go and stop looking for things that are ungodly on the internet.

3. Abnormal objectifying:

This is the process by which we depersonalise an image. You lose sight of the fact that the person in the image is a real person with a life of their own. The person becomes virtual and loses his or her context as a real human being. God had all of this in mind long before the internet and the printing press were about. The Christian viewpoint is that looking at pornography (and anything more involved) is a sexually immoral act. Jesus said, "Whosoever looks at a woman to lust for her has already committed adultery with her in his heart." Whether you are married or not, you are having a false or pseudo-intimacy involving the image you use as you gratify yourself. If you are not married, then the offence is against the woman you will get married to – both amount to the same thing, committing spiritual adultery. Once the addiction takes over, it gratifies and satisfies you in areas of intimacy designated to God and your partner. And that's nothing less than idolatry. The bad coping strategy becomes the idol you cling to in your addiction. Such stubbornness pursuance of your own desires, lusts, fantasies and will to the detriment of God's will amounts to rebellion. "No man can be a slave (servant) of two masters; he will hate one and love the other; he will be loyal to one and despise the other." It's not an all or nothing principle, but constantly living contrary to His plans for you will gradually erode your love for the Lord and you can and will forfeit what He wants for you. It seems like we live in **a virtual world** most of the time. **Social media, social networking, films, television and modern phones make objectifying so much easier**. The person on the screen or in the magazine is de-humanised, objectified and is not a real human being or "person" anymore. There is no real emotional interaction or consideration for the person involved with his or her authentic life and feelings. If you have any consideration, they will be very superficial. Objectification is a very real and major issue in our society today, in our culture we are constantly bombarded with images of a sexual nature, whether they are selling perfume, chocolate, jewellery, holidays or clothes – erotic, sexualised advertisements in magazines, movies and "reality shows" are rife and hedonism is encouraged in many night clubs and bars. The boundaries are blurred and true empathy have drained away and it makes that person in your imagination the mere object of your desire and ultimate gratification. Repeatedly doing so leads you into the addiction and a captivated life built around self-fulfilment in a very negative sense. The industry understands these principles very well, which is why these women are groomed to portray themselves as "being available" and "being there for you", wanting you, caring about you. The truth is they are facing a camera and they are being exploited to feed the consumer's appetite. You will not be aware or informed of the sacrifices some of these women must make in presenting these images to you (drug abuse, intimidation, prostitution or just plain bribery – all of which are demeaning and undermining their self-esteem and self-worth). The callousness grows, objectification doesn't necessarily happen overnight. It slowly dilutes the way we think about people around us and the way we see them and respond to them. It doesn't only do so on a sexual level, but also in a more general way, we start to see people as objects that can fulfil our needs and gratify our desires, even on a spiritual plane.

4. *Lack of intimacy:*

Another issue is the lack of intimacy and/or sex. It can be a breeding ground for trouble. Don't let issues in your marriage relationship create an elephant in the room. Communication is the basis of all relationships. And don't spice up your sex life with pornography, even though the world might condone it, God doesn't! And the enemy will gain a foothold which will be costly in the end. Get good godly counselling in that area if necessary.

Whatever the cause(s) in your life, make sure you get to the root of them, identify the triggers and deal with them effectively. More about how to later.

Internet porn and social media are freely available. The internet is now an integral part of our lives, it's relatively inexpensive, it's interactive; and, more dangerously, it is isolating. You can hide behind a keyboard and a screen and believe that you are invisible; you feel safe and secure. Ultimately, if it's not understood and controlled, it can be intoxicating. The lack of authentic intimacy substituted with an on-demand virtual yet gratifying sexual experience. And that is sad.

5. *Bubbling:*

"Bubbling" is an apt term coined by SAA (Sex Addicts Anonymous) and it describes the moments or episodes where an addict decides to "escape from reality" (originally as a coping mechanism, but later it forms an integral part of the ritual and the addiction). An addict goes into his or her "own little world" for some "relief". Once your behaviour becomes both rewarding and reinforcing the addiction becomes a lifestyle. This might involve web surfing, interacting inappropriately with social media sites, trawling the net - reading, downloading, texting or even phoning. Initially, such isolation and escapism are short-lived, but it will demand more and more of the addict's time and effort as the bubble grows. Apart from damaging yourself and growing more insular, more independent, your relationships will inevitably start to suffer; with God, yourself, your partner or spouse, your family, friends and work colleagues. Because of the addiction and the natural course it takes, you will, in time, put yourself, your reputation, your family, and your job on the line. Once the law is broken, the consequences are dire – not just for yourself, but for all those around you. You could end up with a criminal record.

Consider the consequences of downloading illegal porn:

If any images deemed illegal is found in your possession, you will face a conviction, whether 2, 3, 5, or 5000 images are found. As things stand, a conviction will follow. The law makes no distinction between images you have on your computer (accessible) or those you have deleted (inaccessible). **Do not** rely on your software to **"permanently"** delete any data. The recovery programmes and equipment are *extremely* powerful and effective.

You could and probably will lose your job, your family, and very possibly your home. You will lose your reputation and if you are found guilty, you will certainly become marginalised in Western society. You could face a prison sentence. If you are in the UK and your sentence is longer than 6 months, you will be on the sex offender's register for at least 15 years and you will be constrained socially in ways that you cannot even imagine. Even with a caution, you will be placed on the register for two years. You will pay more for car insurance depending on the provider. Just going to church will be a major issue in terms of disclosure, signing a contract and being chaperoned. Safeguarding policies will preclude you from most ministries and your voice in the church will be quelled.

Stop now, change things while you can. God has a specific dislike for sexual hypocrisy, you are not invisible and you are invincible, and you won't remain hidden. Count the cost, the price is too high!

No man is an island

In Christian terms, we are never alone. Christianity is about community. God in the Trinity is a community. We are not alone. The biggest lie is the belief that we only hurt ourselves, in isolation. The bigger picture is that there are always others involved and affected by the addiction. A "fall-out" if you wish. One should never underestimate the pain, hurt and devastation such addiction will leave in its wake. As it slowly eats away at your character, those around you and anyone who cares about you will be affected. One's active participation in the porn industry fuels more investment and more abuse, and could even passively contribute to the sex trade. Different ages at which different countries allow pornography makes it very probable for a person to eventually or inadvertently download illegal porn (including "child pornography"). Crossing that line will most probably serve as a permanent marker in your life.

Identity, free will and grace:

We are servants or slaves of our own choices. How do we know we are a slave to pornography? When we feel as if we have lost the ability to choose freely whether to stop or continue looking at it. Such out-of-control behaviour will be marked by rituals and the obsession to continue amid feelings of frustration, self-blame, guilt, powerlessness and hopelessness. You're stuck in the hedge when your expectations and associated feelings and thinking processes have become fixated on "the next time". It can be likened to a needle in a record player being stuck in a groove, returning to the same point again and again.

So, the question remains, "Who are you?" If you want to produce apples, you have to plant an apple tree. A bramble does not produce strawberries. This is reflected in the Scriptures as "where your treasure is, there your heart will be also." The cliché is that thoughts and feelings govern our choices, our choices become actions, actions become habits, and habits become our character. So the question remains, "What do you *really* want out of life"? Even though things have become unmanageable, as with any addiction, ***there must be a real will to break free from it***; whether smoking, gambling, alcohol, drug and/or pornography. It might sound superfluous (needless) to say, but it is a core issue. How serious are you deep, deep inside to give up the way you cope with life, the thing you like, the addiction, the buzz that goes with it and the gratification that comes from it? You must *want* to break free from the addiction-shame cycle because you desperately want to. It includes a sincere willingness to step away from that which gratified you and gave you pleasure and a measure of satisfaction and short-lived fulfilment. **All the steps in the world and all the help you can get will not break you free *unless you want to break free in the first place.*** The call is to die to yourself and your own desires and to follow Him and live in His Presence empowered by His grace. The invitation is there, but will *you* respond to it?

Where is God in all of this?

God created us with a free will, we must take responsibility for our actions. That might make God seem aloof, even though I can assure you He is not! What are the steps we must take to draw near to God? Salvation comes from *repentance*, realising you're caught in dead and destructive works, a *changing your mind* and *turning to God*. Accepting the truth that Jesus Christ paid the price for your wrongs and *believing* in Him brings you into right standing with God your eternal Father. Such *faith* is given substance by *confessing aloud* that Jesus has become your Lord Master and God. Your words must reflect your heart. Here we also should consider two traps people might fall into:

   (a) antinomianism - which is just a fancy word for "anything goes, God will eventually forgive it all" or "I know better, I can reject any Biblical and socially established morality" because of God is a God of mercy. After all, Jesus paid for my past, present and future sins (once and for all).

   (b) strict legalism - "God will never accept you while engaging in pornography, gambling or any other addiction". God does not condone sin, but He loves people and He paid the price for all people to be reconciled with Him while they were sinners.

But once we've been reconciled, we should desire to know and love Him better. Paul wrote, "Therefore, I urge you, brothers and sisters, in view of God's mercy, to offer your bodies as a living sacrifice, holy and pleasing to God—this is your true and proper worship. Do not conform (be moulded) to the pattern of this world, but be transformed (change into another form) by the renewing of your mind. Then you will be able to test and approve what God's will is - His good, pleasing and perfect will." Even now, make that choice to honour God. Choose to have a change of heart, a change of mind; and it is possible!

For the addict, please reconsider; for the non-addict, try to understand:

"What we have found really troubling is that many of our clients confide that they are unable to stop using pornography even when they are aware of the negative consequences it is having (and might still have) on their life." (The Porn Trap).

As an addict, you can become deaf and insensitive to the sincere voices trying to turn you around, even now, reading this sincere plea for you. That is because your desire for what you want becomes bigger than the desire to break free. In your heart, your core, you are convinced that you must have the product or gratification of your addiction, you have scaled and broken down necessary boundaries and you have justified what you do to yourself to such an extent that you become very deaf to the truth or the call to change. There is a feeling that nothing else will be able to fill the void as effectively as the addiction, *but I can assure you, you can break free and it is never too late, and there are better things that will make life not only worthwhile but fun and filled with joy.*

It's understandably hard; yes, very difficult to break the addiction cycle; especially if you are not fully convinced that you really want to do so. As one who lost it all, I ask you to at least *consider the worst-case scenario*, think of what is possible, should your addiction run its course. Know and understand the deep, deep hurt and pain such addiction causes God, your spouse or partner, your family and friends as well as others who care for you. Consider the damage you cause yourself as you remain trapped in the cycle of self-gratification and then the shame that ensues afterwards. Once you can see the senseless pain it can cause, it will serve as a strong deterrent. Ask Holy Spirit to make it abundantly clear to you.

Steps to recovery!

1. <u>The first step to recovery</u>:

Acknowledge that your life has become unmanageable and that you have difficulties controlling your desires for pornography, sex or whatever else you're addicted to.

Acknowledge *the fact* that you actually *like* what you do – it gives you gratification, even if it is just for the moment.

Repent anew! Come back to the point where you see the shame-based lifestyle and repent anew. *God will hand persistently disobedient people over to their own desires.* He will intervene in passive ways, but *ultimately, it's up to you* - it is in the nature of free will that *you* should *actively* accept His offer for grace and change. It is His kindness and goodness that should lead us to repentance, to change our minds and to receive a new heart to follow Him. It is a path of dying to yourself and your own wants and to choose to live anew for Him. "*So prepare your minds for action and exercise self-control.* Put all your hope in the gracious salvation that will come to you when Jesus Christ is revealed to the world. So, you must live as God's obedient children. *Don't slip back into your old ways of living to satisfy your own desires.* You didn't know any better then. But now you must be holy in everything (all that) you do, just as God who chose you is holy" (NLT).

2. <u>Don't do this alone!</u>

Rededicate your life with someone else, someone you trust. **Openly confess your sin and *bring it out of the shadows***; a lot of the addiction's power lies in its secrecy.

Once you have repented and disclosed your addiction, seek out the Scriptures that affirm your true identity in Christ Jesus. **Confess regularly that *you are the righteousness of God in Christ***. Acknowledge that it is by grace that you've been saved through faith, not of works. It will deal with the unnecessary guilt entailed with the addiction.

3. <u>Don't become sin conscious</u>

"Try to pose for yourself this task: not to think of a polar bear, and you will see that the cursed thing will come to mind every minute." Psychologist Daniel Wegner, PhD, a psychology professor at Harvard University ran the test and *he confirmed that the negative reinforcement that accompanies "trying not to think of what you shouldn't be thinking about" is extremely powerful.* He proposed several ways of getting rid of the polar bears, one was to pick an **absorbing distractor** and to focus on something else instead. This is the same as Paul's teaching, "whatever is true, whatever is noble, whatever is right, whatever is pure, whatever is lovely, whatever is admirable—if anything is excellent or praiseworthy—think about such things." In real terms, this means you have to develop an alternative coping strategy, habit or active hobby. Painting, writing, sport or past-time. This can form part of another process, which is called sublimation; expressing one's anxiety in socially acceptable ways. Sublimation is a mature type of defence mechanism where socially unacceptable impulses, thoughts or feelings are unconsciously transformed into socially acceptable actions or behaviour, which can possibly result in a long-term conversion of the initial impulse or stimulus. For example, playing more sport or joining a social club. Another way is to acknowledge your behaviour as addictive and channelling it into something more "positive", both Joyce Meyer and Mike Bickle have publicly said that they are "addicted to Christ"; they have used their fervour and zeal in a positive way, and so can you.

4. <u>One day at a time.</u>

Every day is a new day in which to understand who you are and an opportunity to embrace your new identity and life in Christ. You are a child of the Living God, a "son" of Father-God. When He called you to walk in holiness and purity, it was not to try and keep His laws and decrees. *He* promised that He would write His laws in your heart. *He* would give you the grace (the God-ability or God-enablement) to walk it out. ***Your first step in your personal divine relationship is to fall in love with Him and to develop a healthy reverential awe to worship and honour Almighty God***. This shift in life is crucial. It will help you to see what tree you are (figuratively speaking). Once you can see that you are destined for great things in Him, to bear godly fruit, it will become easier to say no to pornography or inappropriate sexual habits. *You can and will overcome when you allow the grace of God to activate your life through the indwelling of Holy Spirit.* The Promise of the Father is there to help you to be an effective witness for Him. That's keeping your eye on your destiny, don't sell your first-born right for a bowl of soup. *The change is inside-out*, a new heart and developing healthy new desires, more fulfilling than pursuing the excitement found in the addiction and concentrating on walking with a pure conscience every step of the way.

5. Rebuilding or raising new boundaries.

This might be as simple as to develop *consequential thinking*. Giving up the short-sighted desire for instant gratification. **The vicious cycle spiralling down into finally falling again into the hands of the addiction has clear signposts along the way**. Proverbs has an analogy where the wayward woman, who represents evil desire, calls you while you're on the road to fulfil your destiny, you then stop at her house; where, after you open the gate, you go down the path to the front door where you then step onto the threshold; and then open the door, where at last you succumb to her whiles. As you develop stronger boundaries or "opt-out" moments it will make each step back to the addictive path more and more difficult to take. At the same time you will have to employ active consequential thinking, regarding each step in the wrong direction as more and more dangerous and destructive. Such a pattern of prudent thinking will eventually help you to break the cycle before it's too late.

It is important, however, to understand that you ended up where you are within the addiction because you didn't honour or keep to God's (and/or society's) boundaries. Boundaries aren't always black and white. In practical terms, this means that some people will have to avoid going onto the internet at all, while others can break the habit by knowing what ritual sets it all off, and then avoiding that. **The boundaries will need to be redefined and relearned for an addict**. As a Christian, you must also cultivate a sensitive conscience and learn to obey Holy Spirit *immediately*. **Do whatever it takes to learn to hear and to discern God's voice.** There are many additional helps out there that can facilitate the process, particularly the workbook by Mark and Patti Virkler, *Hearing the voice of God.*

Still, *there is no substitute for an active prayer life and participation in a vibrant church which gives good pastoral care and mentoring*. If you're on the Sex Offender's register accept the fact that you will be regarded as a second-rate or marginalised Christian in a UK church, because of "safeguarding" you will most probably have to sign a contract with the church.

These personal boundaries are there for you to "see and avoid" any "red-flag" situations, and to encourage and enable you to "walk away" from the path that will lead to your destruction and misery. A good "boundary" starts with understanding your purpose, your life's aim.

You have a destiny in Christ:

Someone once wrote, "All sinners have a future and all saints have a past". And, "Successful people look at where they are going to, rather than where they came from." On the path of death due to the lust or desire for sex or pornography, **it is not enough to say, "I don't want it in my life anymore"**, you need to see its temporal futility and the eternal damage it leaves behind. You have to choose to pursue God's best for you, *"I want what God wants for me. I want to follow Him and do what pleases Him. I want to fulfil my destiny in Him and live a fruitful life in Him. Above all, I want to love Him with a pure and sincere heart, filled with joy and thankfulness."*

Not only is your identity wrapped up in Jesus; God actually has a destiny and a good plan for your life. Each one of us has a specific task or calling on this earth, but it is up to you to embrace His plan and to follow it through. His plans will always be greater and better than the short-lived self-gratifying moments. "I know the plans I have for you, plans to prosper you and to do you good, not to cause disaster or to bring evil upon you, but I have plans to give you a hope and a future." (Jeremiah 29:11)

Now as you overcome step-by-step, day-after-day, you will become a blessing - a blessing to God, to others and to yourself. As much as the addiction negatively impacted your life, so now the turnaround will positively impact you, your relationship with God and all others around you, your community and even your society.

The essence of true repentance: A definite decision for godly change.

It is all about making the right choices! And it starts and finishes with you. You make that choice with Holy Spirit and *you have to say,* "**NO MORE**; Your will be done in my life O Lord." Stay persistent in your desire to overcome. No matter how tough the struggle is or how many times you relapse, "When I fall, I will arise; when I sit in darkness, The Lord will be a light into me. I will bear the indignation of the Lord, Because I have sinned against Him." *You will be able to assume and resume your true identity after you've come to that point of consecration (once you rededicate all of yourself to God).* But you can only get there by a grace-encounter, where you realise that He has paid it all and that it is up to you to accept His love for you in spite of your short-comings by faith.

Then we must recognise that an apple tree produces apples. What fruit are you producing? The scary thing is, "As a tree falls so it will lie", you do not want to die and go into eternity unchanged. *you are who you are* and the fruit you bear will reflect who you are. When addiction to porn and sex form part of your life, then that is inherently who you are at that point in time. Even if you are actually "a nice person", the addiction will dictate how you use your time, your quality of life and the way you manage yourself. That part of "you" will need to be dealt with now. Once you are ready to lay it down and realise it is not who you want to be, you can collaborate with God and fellow workers in God's kingdom to bring about that change. God can and will transform you in and through His love and grace.

1. What's required is change - not superficial, but a change in depth – inside out:

We all want authentic change, not superficial, but a true and sincere change. There must be a change of heart, a relentless pursuit for Him, His kingdom and that inward change (Matthew 6:33). In psychological or secular terms it might be conceived as a transference or conversion reaction (a positive defence mechanism) do *not* be put off by this and/or another form of cynicism by others. **Still, just do what is right, put God first** – He promises, *"Then you will call upon Me and pray to Me, and I will listen to you. And you will seek Me and find Me, when you search for Me with all your heart. I will be found by you, says the Lord"* (NKJV).

This change of heart, mind and soul is called repentance. And it is the foundation for our faith towards God. Believing in the goodness of God and desiring to be the son (or daughter) He wants you to be. Like the prodigal son returning from total devastation. Know that there is so much more and a much better life waiting for you. God's love will continually call you to come, to be healed, to turn around and to embrace the fullness of what He has in store for you.

2. The role of the world and the Enemy.

It is important to understand that, "When tempted, no-one should say, 'God is tempting me'. For God cannot be tempted by evil, nor does He tempt anyone; but each one is tempted when by his (or her) own evil desire (lust), he (or she) is dragged away and enticed (trapped). Then, after desire has conceived, it gives birth to sin, when it is full-grown, gives birth to death." (James 1:13-15).

Make no mistake; on the other hand, the Devil and his demonic hosts will do everything in their power to entice you and to try and lead you astray. The Devil will use the things of this world to entice you, to try and lure you away from God and all godliness and he will help you to *rationalise your situation* and even whisper thoughts to your inner ear, the best of the *"permission-givers"*! You even find that while you're online you will be so "lucky" as you inadvertently stumble on to something that is *not* good for you, or that sets the ritual for the addiction off. If you pass the test and refuse the offer, you will grow stronger and stronger in your ability to recognise and to resist the enemy's temptations. To say no to the world's enticing allure. You must also understand that "the weapons of our warfare are not carnal, but mighty in the pulling down of strongholds, taking captive every thought that works against the knowledge of God and this we will do when *our* obedience is perfect." (2 Corinthians 10:2-5 - NKJV). And, "Submit yourselves therefore to God, resist the devil and he will flee from you" (James 4:7 – NIV) Spiritual warfare always takes place in your mind and with tempting and deceiving thoughts the enemy through a love for the world and its allure will try to capture and recapture your heart. Learn how to take authority and how to deal with the enemy through prayer.

God will enable you to walk with Him and to follow in His ways; He will set the pace and the path if you will let Him. Put on the whole armour of God, please read and meditate on Ephesians 6:10-18.

3. Deal with the past effectively.

"Sexual imprinting" (your very first exposure to sexual activity), "soul-ties" (people you've been intimate with) and "soul-spirit hurts" (spiritual and emotional scars because of painful experiences) can often provide a demonic foothold. *When the addiction is totally out of hand*, seek help, there are particular ministries that are very good and trained to help you and to deal with demonic activity in your life. Be aware that there are such things as "sex-demons" and "unclean spirits". Self-deliverance is the last option, formal and pastoral help from people properly trained and equipped to deal with these matters will prove to be more efficient and invaluable for you.

4. Learn how to protect your heart and mind:

"Keep (or garrison) your heart with ALL diligence, for out of it springs or flows) the issues of life" (Proverbs 4:23). So how do you "keep" or "garrison" your heart? Your heart refers to the core of who you are, like the fruit tree as said before. Jesus said, "out of the heart proceed evil thoughts, murders, adulteries, fornications, thefts, false witness, blasphemies." He was saying that it is not what you physically eat that will defile you, but that our hearts form the core of our being, and that it is the inner change that is crucial, more so than trying to change and control our behaviour without changing who we are in Him. It starts with identifying who you are in Him and then you also must ensure that you only "eat" healthy, proper, spiritual food. ***Once we are resolved to love and serve our God, from a pure heart and a clean conscience, we need to take great care what we feed upon.*** Our physical and spiritual senses work together in taking things on board. We interact with our environment and people through our senses; seeing, hearing, tasting, smelling and touching. Jesus emphasised this in a radical but figurative way, "If your right eye causes you to sin, pluck it out and cast it from you." Not literally, but "whatever you see in your mind's eye". *We tend to look at what we want to look at* or desire to look at, even in the literal or natural sense we will turn our eyes away from "what we do not want to see", e.g. a bad car crash. We have a choice to say "no" and "look away", to "cast" what is in sight, that "eye" away from you. In the same vein, Jesus also said, "take no thought". In the original language it literally means

"to grasp" or "to take hold of" the thought or idea. **In other words, we have moment when we are presented with a thought, an image, an idea or an opportunity, and then we are afforded the choice – a moment of prudence – where we can choose to accept or to reject the idea, image or stimulus we face.**

5. Take no thought!

This is such a useful, personal truth, it's worth exploring a bit more. *The realisation that we have that grace of divine prudence to reject any temptation set before us.* As you observe things around you, you have a choice to accept or reject thoughts, to lock onto things, for instance, an idea, desire or imagination, to make it your own, to take ownership of it. Your eyes are the windows of your heart, your ears are the doors to your heart and your desires regulate the gates to our heart. So, when you are presented with the "lust of the flesh" or the "lust of the eye", then "take no thought", recognise the boundary you have to drop, shut the door and close the window – all in all, refuse to take it on board, reject it as of this world and of the Enemy. Holy Spirit will alert you if you let Him, honour the divine boundaries and guard your heart with all diligence. The sooner you recognise the boundary with its red flags, and you shut the gate and close the window the better. The Enemy might try and use memories of the old desires, gratifying moments and/or inquisitiveness to allure you; but you have to be firm, set yourself some clear, practical boundaries. For instance, if you find a movie sexually charged and having an influence on you, stop watching it, turn to God.tv or TBN, or switch the telly off. Fill your mind and heart with God, seek out His Person and His Kingdom. Say no for Christ's sake -- He redeemed you at great cost, and the way you live in this short life determines how you will live eternally. When you see a scantily clad well-proportioned girl and you feel that excitation in response, immediately ask yourself, "What is she in relation to me?" "In the long run, what lasting effect will she have on my life?" Refuse to objectify! She's real and she's not part of your personal reality – in fact she is nothing to you! In real terms, she's outside of an authentic relationship with you. If anything, just say a prayer for her, bless her and then walk on. If you are married, practical reminders like rubbing your wedding ring, or flicking an elastic wrist-band (also called active distraction) and remind yourself of your solemn commitment before God. Also remind yourself of how this could hurt your wife – imagine the worst-case scenario and realise if you continue with such a pattern what could happen in terms of your relationship with God, your spouse and/or yourself (covert sensitisation). These can be powerful practical ways in which you can overcome the temptation and walk out a new life in Christ.

Always draw God into the situation, after all, He promised, "l will never leave you or forsake you". Paul's exhortation will always stand you in good stead, "pray without ceasing, rejoice at all times and be thankful in all things". Remind yourself that God has promised to make a way for us not to be tested over and above what we can endure.

6. Run without burdens or constraints.

Stay on track, stay on the road God has mapped out for you, "let us lay aside every weight, and the sin which so easily beset (or ensnare) us, let us run with patience the race set before us." *When you fail, don't go on a guilt trip.* Sincerely confess it (preferably to a confidant), repent anew and get back on track as quickly as possible. *Celebrate every step every day as you slowly but surely move forward.* As you do so the road becomes progressively easier, that's a solemn promise!

It is worth quoting 1 Thessalonians 5:15-18 again, "See that no one renders evil for evil to anyone (forgive, forgive and be merciful), but ALWAYS pursue what is good, both for yourselves and for all. Always rejoice and pray without ceasing, and in everything give thanks; for this is the will of God in Christ Jesus for you."

7. A song you won't hear in heaven – "I did it my way".

It of crucial importance not to walk this path on your own, independence will leave you very vulnerable. I pray that you will find a congregation of believers that will practice Galatians 6:1, "Brethren, if a man is overtaken in any trespass (he knew what was wrong and still did it!), you who are spiritual, restore him gently (in a spirit of gentleness)". A non-judgemental, encouraging family of believers. Come into a healthy fellowship and befriend people who will support and encourage you. People, who will love you, yet be honest enough to tell you the truth; that will exhort you, edify you and help you to become the person God always intended you to be. If you can obtain a pastor, mentor or sponsor to whom you can be fully accountable to in the Lord, then do so. They can co-labour with you, have set times to talk and to pray with you and nurture you into a restored life in the Lord.

8. Other helps!

There are now many Christian tools available to help you on this path to complete deliverance and healing, particularly if you have been set up with a predisposing background and unhealthy environment. Books include "Restoring the Foundations" (Chester and Betsy Kylstra); the "Sozo" course developed at Redding USA (Bethel Church with Pastor Bill Johnson); "Freedom in Christ" – Neil Anderson; Elijah House Ministries (Sandfords) and Ellel Ministries in the UK all are all excellent, these life-changing counselling ministries are worthwhile pursuing. Secular help can also be helpful as with the Lucy Faithful Foundation. Use whatever is necessary to aid you on this path of recovery; good sex counsellors and Sex Addicts Anonymous can all prove to be useful on different levels. These helps can help establish that all-important change and sanctifying process, as well as firmly ground you in your true, God-intended identity.

Helpful non-Christian books on the subject are "In the shadows of the net" by Patrick Carnes et al, published by Hazelden; and, "The Porn Trap" by Wendy & Larry Maltz, published by Harper.

<u>In Summary:</u>

Let's recap on some of these important tools which can help you to follow the road to freedom.

1. Make God your priority. Make Him your passion.

Your aim on earth is to become the Bride and wife of Christ, to become one with God. Seek *Him* out, grow in intimacy with Him. Putting your eternal purpose first will help you to stay on course and refuse to sell your inheritance off cheaply.

Prayer, Bible Studies, fellowship, meditation, resting in His presence, worship and communion are but some of the healthy means of growing ever closer to Father God and Jesus through Holy Spirit.

Sexual addiction very often has to do with voids and/or difficulties in understanding and maintaining interpersonal intimacy levels. Developing your eternal intimacy level with God must come first!

a. Attend a healthy church and come into fellowship with the congregation and get your Pastor, Minister or Vicar on board. Be accountable to at least one, but preferably two people whom you can contact at any time. People who are willing to walk with you every step of the way.

b. Ensure you are filled with Holy Spirit and pray in the Spirit as much as possible. Pray in tongues regularly, worship Him continually. Ask Him daily to fill, saturate and inundate you anew with His love and Holy Spirit.

c. Embrace your true identity in Christ. Know who He says who you are in Him. You are the righteousness of God in Christ. You are his beloved child with a purpose and a destiny in Him. Your sins or crimes do not define you. Your relationship with God, yourself and others define you. Getting rid of the addiction and its roots are all part of your walk into a new freedom in Christ (also called progressive sanctification).

d. Actively pursue God and His presence, every day! Be zealous and devoted to entering into His tangible Presence (become aware of His Person being with you wherever you are, wherever you go) and embrace and feel His love. Become more like "Mary" and "be" *with* Him, rather than a "doer" working *for* Him like Martha. Meditate and rest in His wonderful Presence. Soak up His peace, grace and mercy for you, don't hesitate to just "be" and to sit at His feet. His love conquers all!

e. Do regular Bible Study and prayerful journaling.

f. Understand what the will of the Lord is for you. If you are unsure of your calling or destiny, engage people who can help you, there are many trustworthy prophetic voices in the Church.

g. Humble yourself under the mighty hand of God. Walk a walk of daily repentance, recognising the past and it hurts but not living out of them anymore, rather see God's future for you. "The only thing that counts is faith expressing itself through love" (NIV).

h. The analogy is that of "the first minute will determine how the hour will be spent". The quality of your eternal life will be irrevocably determined by how you have lived your life here on earth. Be wise and invest in godliness and holiness and ensures an excellent quality of life for eternity. Be vigilant and determined, keep your eyes on the prize. Run the race to obtain God and His prize.

i. Maintain the joy for your life. The joy of having eternal life with Jesus is a special and real gift. Celebrate its truth in spite of all the setbacks, no matter how many times you've fallen. "Rejoice in the Lord and again I say rejoice" (NKJV). Remember it's not about how many times you've fallen, it's always about will you get up again! Failing is not the biggest issue in life, giving up is!

j. Please, please, please - guard, protect, enshrine your heart with *ALL* diligence. Keep a tender heart and a clean conscience. Avoid all blame-shifting and bitterness. Be quick to forgive and do not keep any accounts, even your own disappointments, just forgive and forgive - those who show mercy will obtain mercy. At all cost avoid any bitterness, anger and unforgiveness (Psalm 37:8).

2. Quell all ungodly curiosity, that urge to "find a better or different one".

Reject the excitement that fuels the addiction, that comes with ungodly discoveries. Be content within your relationships; and if not, apply that curious urge in a creative godly fashion. Develop healthy outlets, paint, write, play sport, but become creative in constructive, even God-inspired ways.

3. Review your coping strategy.

99.9% of the time the addiction will be your main coping strategy. It might be effective in the very short-term, even instantly, but it will leave you worse for wear soon afterwards. Consciously look for an alternative outlet or coping strategy to deal with all of life's stresses and difficulties. As said before, this will be a new personal development.

4. Fast and/or abstain for two weeks.

If possible, and the addiction is strong or prevails, consider fasting for two weeks, or at least abstain from looking at anything remotely to do with pornography for two weeks; but engage a prayer partner's support during that time. You will experience amazing blessings and new-found freedom.

5. Renounce all entitlements and live a life of perpetual thankfulness. Start confessing that *"I am the righteousness of God in Christ"* and/or *"By faith I declare that in Jesus' Name I have been set free from all addictions"*. And thank God for the truth of those statements.

6. Acknowledge the impact and toxic effects of the addiction.

Acknowledge the impact and toxic effects of the addiction to yourself, your relationships with God, your family, friends and society as a whole. You might find it useful to read the 12 Steps of Sex Addicts Anonymous at some time; you can amend it to reflect your Christian beliefs. Pursue holiness, and you will see God.

7. Above all else, "do no harm".

Above all else, "do no harm", be convinced and utterly determined not to cause anyone any unnecessary pain or hurt (and that includes yourself)!

8. Honour boundaries and be very aware of all red flags.

Make a list of every amber and red light situations that would lead you astray, and define them in practical ways. For instance:

(a) Set the computer in an open space where whosoever walks in will see it all.

(b) Deny yourself certain sites that would lead you on to further explore ungodly sites.

(c) Don't drink alcohol and then surf the web!

(d) Don't go on-line when you feel sexually aroused.

Set up all such simple but effective practical measures. Avoid *all* predisposing factors and vulnerable situations or "rituals". Urge surfing can still work here, that means by just refusing to give way to the urge, the desire will wane in time. Set good boundaries and avoid anything that will lead you to "act out" (i.e. masturbate or to have extramarital sex). Say no to sexually charged or explicit movies, magazines or conversations. Again, avoid alcohol, particularly when you are low or alone. Avoid the wrong company and places that could lead you astray. Honour these new boundaries and review them when you fail, recognise your vulnerabilities and protect them.

9. Use any other help that is relevant to keep you free.

Do whatever is necessary to ensure your change is authentic and permanent. **Consider the other ministries and courses** mentioned before: "Restoring the Foundations", "Sozo"; "Ellel", "Freedom in Christ"; and Sex Addicts Anonymous. A particularly good website, dedicated to helping people with porn addiction, is https://www.xxxchurch.com/. It is filled with excellent insights, very good advice, support and monitoring software to help. Well worth a visit!

10. One day at a time!

Continue step-by-step, day-by-day and *just do it*, make the "right" decision, moment by moment - just do what is right at every opportunity. Abhor what is wrong and evil and walk in purity and love.

11. Don't dismiss regular "check-ups".

That is, to go and see Christian counsellors or mentors on a regular basis. Talk to them about your feelings, struggles and celebrate with them your victories. Explore things like your original "imprinting", and ongoing issues that need to be addressed, breaking soul-ties, confessing sins of the fathers, denouncing ungodly beliefs, and get the necessary healing for all soul-spirit hurts and get delivered from all demonic influences. Many churches advocate that their leaders go to such counselling regularly to assess where they are in their walk with the Lord and to ensure that they deal with past and present issues in their life and get the appropriate help before things crop up and cause more serious problems.

12. Destroy all illegal property.

If you are aware of the fact that you have downloaded illegal images, then physically destroy your hard drive. Go to a place where there is an amnesty when you're treated. Anyone treating or ministering to you for downloading illegal images will be considered complicit if they do not disclose your problem to the police both in the UK and in the USA.

If you are willing, there is no better time to take action than NOW. The fact that you have read this book proves your desire for freedom and restoration. And I pray for God's grace to be upon you. Prayerfully work your way through the relevant steps again and again and you will succeed.

If you are a friend or a spouse, keep on praying and do everything in your power to draw the addict out of the shadows of internet porn, then get them to read this book or any book that can help them to be set free in Christ! With Him all things are possible.

Consider the *permanent* fall out of illegal porn once you've been arrested (and convicted):

If you have been arrested and convicted for more than 12 months, you will become an instant leper in this society (UK and USA). You will be permanently marginalised by the law, the police, your workplace (if you can get a job) and even in most churches. The Government has assured that by placing you on the Sex Offenders Register. Safeguarding means that you will never experience mercy in these countries. **You will have incurred the mark of Cain.**

Every authority that can be involved will be involved in your life and your case. **You will be deemed irreparable, irredeemable and incurable.** The truth is that *the fear of sexual reoffending within this society is disproportionate and it is strongly reinforced and driven by mainstream media.* These societies are willing to sacrifice the 96% for the 3-4% that will re-offend. Any "proof" of walking the "right road" will not be recognised as a sure way to recovery, but on the whole, you will be viewed with suspicion due to possible "non-disclosure". Such bias and "safeguarding" will be used as society's excuse to keep you "guilty" or "marked" even though you have not done anything wrong after the full completion of all punishments you've had to suffer for the crime; no matter how long ago it was. That is the stark reality! **You can apply to come off the sex offenders register after a period of 15 years.** This society will refuse to see that you could be or could have been a victim of your own addiction, your own unhealthy coping strategy. This will have to change in time, but *at this point in time the majority of Western Society still cannot grasp the difficulties of physical as well as psychological addictions and the need for rehabilitation and restoration of the people involved.* The psychiatric classification will now consider gambling addiction as a mental health issue. Odd that on the whole porn addiction is considered as entirely different from gambling, alcohol or even drug addiction. In these societies you will be labelled for life. In time, if it is possible, you might have to *consider relocating to another country*, not to re-offend, but to find a life worth living, where you will be valued for who you truly are – a first-class Christian who have changed and willing to make a meaningful contribution to a society that will also honour and respect you for the necessary positive changes you have made in your life. And that brings us to another point. **Your crime does not define you.** Particularly once you have acknowledged its wrongs and have decided to follow a new path and you are willing to embrace change in Him. You <u>can</u> change and <u>will</u> change; the vast majority of psychologist and psychiatrist say so and more importantly our God (and His Bible) says so. *You are defined by Him* and not your fall, the fact that you are getting up and walking again is testimony to this.

God bless you in your walk to freedom and complete victory. I hope and pray that this book will strengthen you in your resolve and ability to permanently break free from the stronghold of addiction in your life.

"Tough times don't last, tough people do." [Please do!]

(Robert Schuller)

Bibliography.

1. Anderson, Neil T; Goss Steve. *Freedom in Christ: Workbook: A 13-week course for every Christian (Freedom in Christ Course)*. Monarch Books; 2009.

2. Carnes, Patrick; Delmonico, David; Griffin, Elizabeth; Moriarity, Joseph; *In the Shadows of the Net. Breaking free of Compulsive Online sexual behaviour*. Hazelden. 2007.

3. Kylstra Chester and Betsy, *An Integrated Approach to Healing Ministry: A Guide to Receiving Healing and Deliverance from Past Sins, Hurts, Ungodly Mindsets and Demonic Oppression*. Sovereign World. 2014.

4. Maltz, Wendy and Larry. *The Porn Trap: The Essential Guide to Overcoming Problems Caused by Pornography*; Harper Paperbacks; 2010.

Printed in Great Britain
by Amazon